Magic Tree Houses

Thank you for purchasing our coloring book!
We hope you have fun and learn a few new things while coloring.
Everyone who contributed to this book appreciates your support.
Please leave a review and shore some of your beautiful
I colored pictures on our amazon page.

Patricia Publishing

this book belongs to

9 798378 619474